ABRAHAM (BIBLE STUDY LEADERS EDITION)

ABRAHAM (BIBLE STUDY LEADERS EDITION)

Biblical Characters Series

JAMES G WHITELAW

Swackie Ltd

CONTENTS

Introduction		1
1	Call and Migration	3
2	Stumbling in the Faith	10
3	Fresh Start	14
4	Parting of the Ways	17
5	The Renewed Promise	21
6	Into Battle	25
7	A Son Promised	30
8	The Covenant	34
9	Shortcuts in the Faith	38
10	Circumcision	41
11	The promise of a Son Affirmed	45
12	The Angels	48
13	Destruction of Sodom and Gomorrah	52
14	The Great Man Stumbles Again	57

15	The Birth of Isaac	61
16	The Ishmael Problem	64
17	The Great Test	68
18	Death of Sarah	72
19	A Wife for Isaac	76
20	Abraham's Death	83
Author's Note		86

Introduction

Introduction

Please note: Throughout this book, I will refer to our subject as Abraham for simplification, although his name was originally Abram and later changed to Abraham. I will also refer to Sarah throughout, although her name was originally Sarai

The story of Abraham is a journey through life. It is a journey all of us are called to make. The circumstances may be different, the location most certainly will not be the same route as Abraham took, but the journey we take will face the same problems and same distractions which would seek to sideline us. Therefore, it is crucial to study these characters. As Solomon said, "Nothing is new under the sun". We can learn from these scriptures, which God has provided for us.

Abraham starts his life in Ur of the Chaldeans, a godless place, and this is where we all start. We come into this life as sinners, and we must begin our journey there. Most people stay there, but some are called to start a journey. When Abraham reached Haran, he settled but was never going to stay there. Haran is Abraham's decision point, and we also will face a moment when we have to decide if we will press on towards the promised land or ignore the call of God.

Abraham then journeys towards and arrives in the promised land but can only see it by faith. He does not possess it at this point but believes God will fulfil his promise. We, too, will own nothing in this world as our sights should be set way beyond earthly realms. God has promised us the same reward as Abraham, and we must keep that in sight as we move through our earthly journey.

We should note that Abraham was called to leave his land, his family, and his homeland. We do not know what God will ask us to do, but you can be sure there will be sacrifices to make along the way, and we must be ready to make them. We must be prepared to lay aside everything that would burden us in our journey.

When Abraham arrives in Shechem, he builds his first altar, and we also must build an altar and make a sacrifice, but Abraham then moves on to Bethel, which in Hebrew means 'House of God'. Likewise, building our first altar and making a sacrifice is not the end for us. We need to press on until we reach the House of God. The House of God is where we must be found.

In the Bible Study Leader's Edition(BSLE), we add extra content and questions for exploration. We suggest points to pause and ponder what has been covered. Although designed for the leader of a small Bible study group, it may be used by an individual seeking a deeper study of the character. There are many questions throughout the book. Give your group the opportunity to answer, but be prepared to take it forward.

Each member of the group should have their own copy of the main book so that they can revise and study between the group gatherings. Any group who do not have the resources, please contact me through my author's website at the end of the book and we will try to help.

CHAPTER 1

Call and Migration

Call and Migration
Genesis Ch11 v 27 to Ch 12 v 9

This is the account of Terah's family line.
Terah became the father of Abram, Nahor and Haran. And Haran became the father of Lot. While his father Terah was still alive, Haran died in Ur of the Chaldeans, in the land of his birth. Abram and Nahor both married. The name of Abram's wife was Sarai, and the name of Nahor's wife was Milkah; she was the daughter of Haran, the father of both Milkah and Iskah. Now Sarai was childless because she was not able to conceive.

Terah took his son Abram, his grandson Lot son of Haran, and his daughter-in-law Sarai, the wife of his son Abram, and together they set out from Ur of the Chaldeans to go to Canaan. But when they came to Harran, they settled there.

Terah lived 205 years, and he died in Harran.

The Lord had said to Abram, "Go from your country, your people and your father's household to the land I will show you. I will make you into a great nation, and I will bless you; I will make your name great, and you will be a blessing. I will bless those who bless you, and whoever curses you I will curse; and all peoples on earth will be blessed through you."

So Abram went, as the Lord had told him; and Lot went with him. Abram was seventy-five years old when he set out from Harran. He took his wife Sarai, his nephew Lot, all the possessions they had accumulated and the people they had acquired in Harran, and they set out for the land of Canaan, and they arrived there.

Abram traveled through the land as far as the site of the great tree of Moreh at Shechem. At that time the Canaanites were in the land. The Lord appeared to Abram and said, "To your offspring I will give this land." So he built an altar there to the Lord, who had appeared to him.

From there he went on toward the hills east of Bethel and pitched his tent, with Bethel on the west and Ai on the east. There he built an altar to the Lord and called on the name of the Lord.

Then Abram set out and continued toward the Negev.

It wasn't a whole lot different from today, to be honest. The world was corrupt, and men were evil! God had flooded the world to rid it of wicked men, and then he had scattered them by confusing their tongues while they were building the tower of Babel. It had made no difference, so now God was going to do something different. God had decided to make a people for Himself, a people whom he would communicate with and bless with abundance.

BSLE: Consider how corrupt our world is today, yet God does not send a flood, does not send down fire like he did on Sodom. Is our world today really more corrupt than it has ever been?

This point in the scriptures is the true start of the Bible's story, two thousand years after creation. This is where God's work of redemption begins. Beginning with one man, God builds a nation that will be a blessing to the entire world by bringing forth a redeemer who is willing and able to reconcile us to God.

BSLE: Take a minute to ponder the timing. The first 11 chapters of Genesis cover roughly 2,000 years. The remainder of the Bible cover another 2,000 years and now a further 2,000 years have elapsed. Is this significant?

Abraham was the man whom God had chosen, and it appears that Abraham was chosen because he was upright and good compared to the rest of the population, who were Godless and evil. This does not mean that Abraham would be perfect. Abraham would still make mistakes and stumble as we shall see as we go through this study of his character, but God, in His divine providence, had chosen Abraham as the founder of his people.

God had not chosen Abraham to receive an exclusive blessing. He tells Abraham that all the nations of the earth would be blessed through him. Abraham would merely be the channel of the blessing that would be across the entire world. With hindsight, it easy to study the Bible and for us to see how this promise unfolds over the following two thousand years, but for Abraham, it was a massive leap of faith, and this is what endeared him to God, his faith. At other places in the scripture, we are told that Abraham's faith was credited to him as righteousness. Faith is what matters most to God. In first Samuel 22 v 15, Samuel tells Saul faith that leads to obedience is much better than sacrifice.

BSLE: Consider the extent of God's Church throughout the world. This is the working out of God's promise that all the nations of the earth would be blessed because of Abraham.

Abraham was a great man of faith, one of the heroes of the faith in Hebrews chapter twelve, but as we will see throughout this study, sometimes his faith wavers and leads him into trouble.

The first call on Abraham is a massive request, asking him to leave all his family and his homeland and travel thousands of miles to a place he knew nothing about. It was a huge commitment as little would have been known about anywhere outside their immediate area. It could have been a journey fraught with danger, and there were indeed no actual examples of similar episodes to encourage him.

BSLE: Get out a map of the Middle East, preferably showing the terrain and desert region. Trace the journey Abraham and his family took as you read the next section.

Initially, Terah, Abraham's father and Abraham's nephew accompanied him, and the Bible is silent on why they all went. As far as we know, only Abraham received the call. We would assume that Lot was still a minor, and his grandfather had taken responsibility for him. They reached a place called Haran, which would only be around halfway to their destination, and they settled there. Terah died here, and Abraham then assumed responsibility for Lot, his nephew. There is a school of thought that Abraham's father, Terah, was godless and did not share Abraham's faith, so this was the reason why the journey was not completed until he died.

Abraham is then called to continue his journey, and it would seem they are considerably richer with much more goods and flocks to think about now. At this time, God promises Abraham that he will be greatly blessed and inherit the land to which they are destined. Once again, when they arrive in the land, God reaffirms that this land will be the possession of Abraham's descendants, and Abraham responds by building an altar and worshipping God.

Building altars becomes a theme of Abraham's life, and wherever he goes, usually his first task is to build an altar and to present thanksgiving to God on whom he has come to trust fully. Whether we are just setting off on our Christian journey or we are well along the road, we need to remind ourselves that our first duty to God is to build an altar and worship him. The first item on the Westminster Catechism is "Man's chief end is to glorify God, and to enjoy him forever."

BSLE: Perhaps a good time to take a break and praise God for his goodness and for bringing us into Abraham's family by adoption.

Abraham had arrived in the promised land, and to be honest, there wasn't much to excite anyone. He didn't own a single square foot of it at that point, and other people were living there who had a claim to the land. It all looked impossible, but we have a God who operates in the realm of the impossible. We have a God who makes the impossible possible.

Many things in our lives may seem impossible, but we are called to exercise the same faith Abraham showed. Faith is taking God at his word, acting on it and looking eagerly for the results. We would do well to note that Abraham never saw the fulfilment of his promise in his lifetime. When he died, he only owned one field and a cave as a burial ground, yet he had complete faith in God's promise to his descendants. Indeed, the fulfilment of this promise has still not been fully implemented, but we have seen enough to realise that God is still working out his plan, and we know that he will complete it.

BSLE: Pause for a moment. Ask your group to tell of any items they have been praying for a long time. Pray as a group for these things, acknowledging that God is wiser than us and will deliver in his time.

We should also be ready to step outside our comfort zone. God may well call us somewhere we do not know, something we don't know anything about or do things we are fearful of for different reasons. Our response must always be the same as Abraham. Get up and go! Just do it! If we stop to reason things out, our focus comes off God and onto earthly things. Much of what God asks will never make sense from a temporal perspective. We must obey and leave God to deal with the details. This is the only way we will be effective and profitable servants.

BSLE: Ask your small group if they have felt the call of God at any time. Discuss in what ways the call of God can come. Encourage your group to commit to God's call.

The story of Abraham is a journey through life. It is a journey all of us are called to make. The circumstances may be different, the location most certainly will not be the same route as Abraham took, but the journey we take will face the same problems and same distractions which would seek to sideline us. Therefore, it is crucial to study these characters. As Solomon said, "Nothing is new under the sun". We can learn from these scriptures, which God has provided for us.

Abraham starts his life in Ur of the Chaldeans, a godless place, and this is where we all start. We come into this life as sinners, and we must begin our journey there. Most people stay there, but some are called to start a journey. When he reached Haran, he settled but was never going to stay there. Haran is Abraham's decision point, and we also will face a moment when we have to decide if we will press on towards the promised land or ignore the call of God.

Maybe you are reading this book, and you have never yet decided to follow Christ. Perhaps you have never chosen to begin your journey with Jesus Christ. You are not reading this book by chance. God's spirit is seeking you out and wants you in his kingdom. Lay down this book now, close your eyes and ask Jesus to come into your life and begin your journey today. You may never have another opportunity.

BSLE: Ask your group to briefly tell the story of their decision and identify any who have yet to make the decision. Offer to pray with them and help them make the decision.

Abraham then journeys towards and arrives in the promised land but can only see it by faith. He does not possess it at this point but believes God will fulfil his promise. We, too, will own nothing in this world as our sights should be set way beyond earthly realms. God has promised us the same reward as Abraham, and we must keep that in sight as we move through our earthly journey.

We should note, too, that Abraham was called to leave his land, his family, and his homeland. We do not know what God will ask us to do, but you can be sure there will be sacrifices to make along the way, and we must be ready to make them. We must be prepared to lay aside everything that would burden us in our journey.

BSLE: Have any of your group had to make sacrifices? Probe for any who may be struggling with necessary sacrifices.

When Abraham arrives in Shechem, he builds his first altar, and we also must build an altar and make a sacrifice, but Abraham then moves on to Bethel, which in Hebrew means 'House of God'. Likewise, building our first altar and making a sacrifice is not the end for us. We need to press on until we reach the House of God. The House of God is where we must be found.

BSLE: Have a general discussion with your group about this chapter. Ask if there is any part they have not understood. Discuss individual journeys past or future, including any vision your group may have for the future. Write down any vision for future encouragement. Encourage your group to write down their vision and often refer to their vision.

Finally, encourage your group to read the next chapter before meeting again.

CHAPTER 2

Stumbling in the Faith

Stumbling in the Faith
Genesis Ch 12 v 10 to 20

Now there was a famine in the land, and Abram went down to Egypt to live there for a while because the famine was severe. As he was about to enter Egypt, he said to his wife Sarai, "I know what a beautiful woman you are. When the Egyptians see you, they will say, 'This is his wife.' Then they will kill me but will let you live. Say you are my sister, so that I will be treated well for your sake and my life will be spared because of you."

When Abram came to Egypt, the Egyptians saw that Sarai was a very beautiful woman. And when Pharaoh's officials saw her, they praised her to Pharaoh, and she was taken into his palace. He treated Abram well for her sake, and Abram acquired sheep and cattle, male and female donkeys, male and female servants, and camels.

But the Lord inflicted serious diseases on Pharaoh and his household because of Abram's wife Sarai. So Pharaoh summoned Abram. "What have you done to me?" he said. "Why didn't you tell me she was your wife? Why did you say, 'She is my sister,' so that I took her to be my wife? Now then, here is your wife. Take her and go!" Then Pharaoh gave orders about Abram to his men, and they sent him on his way, with his wife and everything he had.

After reading the last stirring chapter, you may be feeling a failure. Perhaps you think I could never attain the standard of faith Abraham had. This chapter will show you that faith is never a straightforward journey. It is never a switch that we flip, and the job is done. We must continue to develop our faith, or whenever we let down our guard and stop trusting in God to deliver, we will stumble as Abraham does here.

BSLE: Discuss if any of the group has stumbled. Use your discretion as to how far you can take this discussion in your group or if you should come back to it on a one-to-one basis later.

God had told Abraham to journey thousands of miles across a desert region, and Abraham had the faith to obey the voice of God and act on this command. God had made some tremendous promises to Abraham, and Abraham believed these promises. It isn't long before Abraham faces his first test, having now arrived in the promised land.

BSLE: What promises do each of the group hold on to?

If we are to do the work of God, we will need a strong faith, and a strong faith only comes by our faith being tested and tried, and often failing. At times, our failures break us, and we fade away, but at other times, our disappointments make us into stronger characters than ever. Abraham is faced with his first real test here as a famine sweeps over the land.

Having traversed a desert region successfully and being blessed by the hand of God and prospering in an abundance of everything, so much that he worshipped God for his blessing, Abraham now fails to see how God can support him in a famine.

BSLE: How do each group struggle to see how God can provide for us?

The clear call to Abraham was to go to the land of Canaan and settle there. There was no call to move on again, and indeed, he was to stay in the territory and inherit it. In abandoning the call of God, Abraham was not only showing a lack of faith but also disobedience to the explicit call of God. It was also a challenge and denial of the capabilities of God, implying that God was not able to supply his needs in this land.

As Abraham leaves the House of God and travelled down to Egypt, he was outside God's will, and I guess he knew deep down that he could not rely on the protection of God in this situation, so he took matters into his own hands by creating a deception. Abraham devised a concocted story that Sarah, his wife, was his sister. Sarah was a very beautiful woman, and they were not long in Egypt before Pharaoh heard of her beauty and came looking for her to add to his harem.

BSLE: Have any of the group ever left God's house(backslidden)? Share experiences if they are not too private or revealing.

Even at this point, Abraham said nothing and accepted gifts from Pharaoh because of his good favour. This was never going to end well, and God had to intervene to resolve the situation. He did this by striking the household of Pharaoh with great plagues. When Pharaoh discovered the truth, he was furious at Abraham for his deception and expelled him from the land.

BSLE: Is it our experience that we keep digging deeper holes and get ourselves into bigger messes?

In my own life, I have noticed that I find it easy to believe God can renew my life and absolve me of my sins, but I struggle when I must depend on God for some of the more minor requirements of life. I think it is a case of thinking that we cannot rely on God for everything and do some things for ourselves. This, however, is not God's way. God wants us to depend on him for everything. Indeed he has promised he will supply all our needs. Be careful here, though, to note that needs and wants are two different things. He has not promised to provide everything we want.

BSLE: What is the difference between needs and wants?

When we do go down this route in our own lives, and we all do it, and everyone reading this book will know where he or she has fallen back in this way, it inevitably leads us into a deeper and deeper hole and often needs a big shock to send us back to dependence on God.

Abraham leaves the House of God at Bethel and journeys to Egypt, always portrayed as the world, in the Bible. He is moving from the place of God to the place of Satan, so it is little surprise that it all ends in tears. Satan is the master and creator of chaos, and whenever we go down into Egypt, we can expect the same result.

The big trouble for a Christian going back into the world is that you just don't fit there anymore. You can't settle there and can't be happy there. There are only two options for a Christian in the world. Give up and waste your life or get up and go right back to the House of God. This is precisely what Abraham did.

BSLE: Discuss this chapter in general and probe for any part not understood. Schedule private time with your students over any issue which cannot be discussed in the group. Make a note of any student who needs help and add it to your own personal prayer list.

Finally, encourage your group to read the next chapter before meeting again.

CHAPTER 3

Fresh Start

Fresh Start
Genesis Ch 13 v 1-4

So Abram went up from Egypt to the Negev, with his wife and everything he had, and Lot went with him. Abram had become very wealthy in livestock and in silver and gold.

From the Negev he went from place to place until he came to Bethel, to the place between Bethel and Ai where his tent had been earlier and where he had first built an altar. There Abram called on the name of the Lord.

When we fail, and when we drift away from God, we inevitably come to a place where we are not comfortable or where everything is just getting out of our control. When I have failed God on a number of times, my experience in life is that a sharp shock takes us back to God or the gnawing in our consciences can no longer be quietened. This is the Holy Spirit urging us and leading us back to God.

Whatever the result, it should be noted that there are no incidences in Scripture of God casting off his people. God went over and beyond to redeem us, and Jesus said, "No man will pluck them out of my hand". God will not let us go and let us fall any longer than is necessary to teach us the lessons we need to learn. When the time is right, the Holy Spirit will start drawing us back to God, and the urging will become stronger and stronger until we can no longer ignore it.

There are many examples of this in scripture, and the few verses we read above are one such example. Abraham, at this time, got a sharp short shock when Pharaoh expelled him from Egypt and was pretty much in a position that he had nowhere else to go but turn back to where he last met God. In verse eight of the previous chapter, Abraham built an altar and called upon the name of the Lord. Since then, it had gone wrong, so there was nothing else for it but to retrace his steps and go back to where he had met God and put things right.

BSLE: Discuss times of refreshing among members who have returned to God after failure. Discuss God's faithfulness and how he never gives up on us. Share experiences of God's urging on us.

If we are embarking on the Christian life, we may well be up on the mountaintop, but be assured that valleys will come, and our faith will stumble. It is the only way to learn and grow. When we struggle and eventually come to our senses, then make as fast a return as possible to the last place we met with God. Like the prodigal son, you will find that the father has been watching out for you for a long time and has still reserved the best for you.

God's love for us does not diminish when we fail him. He already knew we were going to do that before he redeemed us. He loved us from the start, knowing how poor we would be, but determined to work on us and build us into a people fit for his kingdom. We will continue to fail all our lives, but when the final curtain falls, we will be perfect and understand all that has gone before is part of the grand plan of God.

BSLE: How many times will God forgive us and draw us back to himself before he gives up on us?

When we return to God, we must, once again, build up the altar, offer our lives as a living sacrifice to Him and strive to live entirely within his will. This is the only place where we can be completely happy as a Christian. Once we have tasted sweet communion with our Lord, nothing else satisfies.

BSLE: Discuss the chapter in general and address any concerns or parts that are not fully understood. This has been a short chapter, and you may have gone through it quite fast. Use any remaining time to praise God for his goodness and faithfulness. Be thankful for any time we have experienced a fresh start.

Finally, encourage your group to read the next chapter before meeting again.

CHAPTER 4

Parting of the Ways

Parting of the Ways
Genesis Ch 13 v 5 to 13

Now Lot, who was moving about with Abram, also had flocks and herds and tents. But the land could not support them while they stayed together, for their possessions were so great that they were not able to stay together. And quarreling arose between Abram's herders and Lot's. The Canaanites and Perizzites were also living in the land at that time.

So Abram said to Lot, "Let's not have any quarreling between you and me, or between your herders and mine, for we are close relatives. Is not the whole land before you? Let's part company. If you go to the left, I'll go to the right; if you go to the right, I'll go to the left."

Lot looked around and saw that the whole plain of the Jordan toward Zoar was well watered, like the garden of the Lord, like the land of Egypt. (This was before the Lord destroyed Sodom and Gomorrah.) So Lot chose for himself the whole plain of the Jordan and set out toward the east. The two men parted company: Abram lived in the land of Canaan, while Lot lived among the cities of the plain and pitched his tents near Sodom. Now the people of Sodom were wicked and were sinning greatly against the Lord.

How often have we seen quarrelling in Churches, so bad that the Churches have split up? I have seen and heard of quite a few in my times, which is usually not very nice. We read about it in the New Testament also, and the Apostle Paul had to address this a few times. It should, therefore, come as no great surprise to us that away back at the dawn of God building his people, there was the same disruption. Satan is always looking for an angle to make God's people less effective.

BSLE: Have any members of the group experience this in practice?

I cannot imagine that Abraham truly wanted to be separated from Lot, but the logistics of staying together were not workable, and something had to be done. Both Abraham and Lot had been so abundantly blessed that the area which they were in was too small for their growing herds. Abraham would have known that Lot would have wavered in his faith without Abraham at his side. He would have known that Lot's faith did not go as deep as his own.

Abraham tries to be as reasonable as can be and offers Lot the first pick of the land. On the one hand, Abraham had learned a lesson that God could bless him and prosper him just as well in a desert as in a lush valley, so it was academic which way he went. On the other hand, Lot had not learned that lesson and could only see the worldly advantage of settling in Jordan's lush valley.

BSLE: In our experiences, were there some gracious people involved?

It is evident that Lot was a selfish person as the custom of that time, more so than today, was always to defer to the senior member of the household. Lot should have declined to choose and let Abraham choose first as the elder of the two. The choice reveals much about Lot's character, and from here on, I think it is fair to say that Lot is a worry to Abraham.

BSLE: Were there selfish people involved?

Quarrels and differences of opinion will happen in our lives and within our Churches. What is the best way to deal with these things?

Strangely enough, we do not read about either of the two taking the matter to God. This should be our first step, to pray about it. If we can pray together about it, so much the better. When we sit down in prayer with a brother, it is exceedingly difficult to talk to God and be selfish when we are reminded in whose name we are making our requests. It is almost impossible to pray through the name of our Lord Jesus, knowing how he selflessly died for us and make selfish requests of our own.

BSLE: How easy is it to take our requests to God when we are angry, feel let down or are sad at some event? How easy is it to pray with the other party?

We can also look toward positive splits in the Bible to see how God can use these things to further his Kingdom and for his glory. A good example is when the early Church faced stiff opposition and persecution. It was taken to God in prayer many times, and God used it miraculously. The split was within God's will, agreeable to all and resulted in the establishment of Churches all over the middle east, where it had previously been concentrated in Jerusalem.

We can also look to the partnership between Paul and Barnabas. After their first missionary journey, where Paul says that John Mark had abandoned them, there arose a dispute when Barnabas wanted to take John Mark with them on the second missionary journey. Paul resisted this, resulting in a split with them both going their separate ways and both being successful.

BSLE: If this group grew too big and we had to split it, would that be a good thing? Would it cause some problems?

The dispute we are looking at today, however, is different. One of the characters was weak and self-centred, and this would lead to many problems for both men as we move forward in the story. Abraham had learned at every step, even from his mistakes. Lot, it seems, had learned nothing and would continue to make bad decisions.

Sometimes in life, disputes will be beyond our control, and distancing is the only solution. This does not mean the end of the relationship, nor the end of any problems associated with the relationship. The one thing that must remain constant in our lives is our relationship to God, and all other issues should be talked over with him. Failure to do this will always mean going our own way and slipping away from communion with God.

BSLE: Discuss the chapter in general and ensure that everyone understands every part of it.

Move on to discuss our priorities. Which place does God take in our lives? If we are asked to give up everything in our lives for his cause, would we do it?

Finally, encourage your group to read the next chapter before meeting again.

CHAPTER 5

The Renewed Promise

The Renewed Promise
Genesis Ch 13 v 14 to 18

The Lord said to Abram after Lot had parted from him, "Look around from where you are, to the north and south, to the east and west. All the land that you see I will give to you and your offspring forever. I will make your offspring like the dust of the earth, so that if anyone could count the dust, then your offspring could be counted. Go, walk through the length and breadth of the land, for I am giving it to you."

So Abram went to live near the great trees of Mamre at Hebron, where he pitched his tents. There he built an altar to the Lord.

With Lot gone, it would seem that Abraham is more focused on God. Could it be that Lot was a distraction to Abraham, and it is only now that he is gone that Abraham is close enough to God that God comes down and talks with him again?

BSLE: have we noticed that the companions we keep, influence us?

God repeats his promise to Abraham and adds some more to it. He asks Abraham to claim the land by walking through it physically. All the land he sees in his travels is to belong to his offspring forever. Also, he promises Abraham that his offspring will be like the dust of the earth, totally uncountable. Abraham responds in his usual manner. He builds an altar and worships the God of heaven.

BSLE: Is it our experience that when we give up something in our lives, make a sacrifice for God's work, that we are blessed and led into a deeper relationship with God?

It seems to me that God made a promise to Abraham, and Abraham has acted and made the journey to the promised land, but beyond that has done little to lay claim to the promise. Barely had he arrived in the land when he left to go down to Egypt. This shows that the promise did not mean enough to him, or he would have remained in the land that God had given to him and not run away.

He returned because he was forced to, but his time was then taken up with day-to-day issues and disputes. God repeats and expands the promise to him and expands what he requires. He expects Abraham to go through all the land and claim it. It seems logical that Abraham needs to see the land to visualise his inheritance, but how often have we been in similar situations and done the same thing as Abraham. We tend to carry on with everyday life and see how things develop, but things never develop as we are not staking our claim with that attitude.

We want to see things happen in our lives. We want to see great things done in God's Kingdom. Perhaps even God has made us a great promise, yet nothing seems to be happening. Could this be because we have not stepped out in faith? Could it be that we have not laid claim to the land?

BSLE: Has God spoken to us? Recall earlier discussion about how God speaks to us. What have we done about the calling? Are we stepping out in faith?

After this, Abraham moves his tent and builds another altar, but there is still no narrative of him walking out the land, claiming it as his own. In hindsight, it is easy for us to see that if we are to be given everything we see, then let's see as much as we can, but perhaps it is not so simple at the time. After all, God gives us the same promise. In John 14 v 13, Jesus says, "Whatever you ask in my name, that will I do, that the Father may be glorified". How much movement does that inspire in us?

There are two schools of thought at play here, and I will leave you to choose which one you think is most appropriate to your situation

1. God has made you a promise, so it will come to pass regardless of your input.
2. God has made you a promise, so you must put 100% effort into working out that promise.

We are always called to walk the land before we see the promise fulfilled, which is true in the secular world and the spiritual world. How often do we pray to God for a revival? If God were to give us a revival suddenly, what would we do with the people who are flocking to our Churches looking for teaching?

If we are praying to God for revival, we need to walk the land. We need to be expecting a result, and if we are expecting a result, we need to be ready. If we have no discipleship classes set up, we are not prepared. If we are not prepared, then we do not expect a result, and our faith is worthless.

We will see no promises fulfilled in our Christian walk until we start walking the land. If we want to see revival in our country, let us begin praying for it. If we start praying for it, let us start believing we will be granted our prayers. If we are believing, let us begin preparing for it.

BSLE: Ideally, before the study, gather some information on previous revivals in your area or country. Pay particular attention to events leading up to the revival. Ask your group if they have heard reports of any prior revival?

Discuss the entire chapter and revival, what we should expect, and what precedes it?

Finally, encourage your group to read the next chapter before meeting again.

CHAPTER 6

Into Battle

Into Battle
Genesis 14 v 11 to 24

The four kings seized all the goods of Sodom and Gomorrah and all their food; then they went away. They also carried off Abram's nephew Lot and his possessions since he was living in Sodom.

A man who had escaped came and reported this to Abram the Hebrew. Now Abram was living near the great trees of Mamre the Amorite, a brother of Eshkol and Aner, all of whom were allied with Abram. When Abram heard that his relative had been taken captive, he called out the 318 trained men born in his household and went in pursuit as far as Dan. During the night Abram divided his men to attack them and he routed them, pursuing them as far as Hobah, north of Damascus. He recovered all the goods and brought back his relative Lot and his possessions, together with the women and the other people.

After Abram returned from defeating Kedorlaomer and the kings allied with him, the king of Sodom came out to meet him in the Valley of Shaveh (that is, the King's Valley).

Then Melchizedek king of Salem brought out bread and wine. He was priest of God Most High, and he blessed Abram, saying,

> *"Blessed be Abram by God Most High,*
> *Creator of heaven and earth.*
> *And praise be to God Most High,*
> *who delivered your enemies into your hand."*

Then Abram gave him a tenth of everything.

The king of Sodom said to Abram, "Give me the people and keep the goods for yourself."

But Abram said to the king of Sodom, "With raised hand I have sworn an oath to the Lord, God Most High, Creator of heaven and earth, that I will accept nothing belonging to you, not even a thread or the strap of a sandal, so that you will never be able to say, 'I made Abram rich.' I will accept nothing but what my men have eaten and the share that belongs to the men who went with me—to Aner, Eshkol and Mamre. Let them have their share."

It's strange. Abraham hesitated and stumbled over small things, yet here we have an example where Abraham did not stop to consider the odds against him but just plunged straight into the pursuit of these kings who had taken away his nephew. There is no mistaking, these kings were formidable and had already defeated a force superior to Abraham's army. However, God was with Abraham, and as we have seen many times throughout the Old Testament, with God, it is not numbers that count. It is faith.

The general process of thought today is that if it doesn't concern you, don't get involved. If someone chooses to go the wrong way, then the consequences are upon their head. We do not risk our resources and family trying to help those not helping themselves, indeed, who have disregarded our help in the past.

BSLE: Do we see people in trouble who worshipped with us? How should we deal with them? Should we be concerned about them?

That is not the Christian way. Imagine if God had taken that attitude with us. What hope would we have? Romans 5v8 says, "But God demonstrates his own love for us in this: While we were still sinners, Christ died for us." Unless God was prepared to get involved with us, who had spurned his love and his grace, we would have had no hope.

This seems to have been the response of Abraham also. Lot had largely forgotten Abraham. We do not hear of them having any communication since they parted company, yet Abraham cared for Lot just as our Father in heaven cares for us. Abraham was prepared to go to extraordinary lengths to rescue Lot and his family.

BSLE: How far would we be willing to go to help a fallen brother or sister who was no longer with us?

If we examine the map of this area, we will find that Abraham pursued this army as much as one hundred and fifty miles. To undertake this mission, succeed and return without casualty or loss is nothing short of miraculous.

In our Christian lives, formidable battles will come before us at some point. The last thing we should do is consider our own abilities. The only question we need to ask is, "Is this of the Lord?" If it is, then we leave the details and outcome to him. There are numerous examples of this throughout the Old and New Testament, and it is because of battles like this, when great victories are won, that great heroes of the faith come forth.

We live in a world today that is just as evil as the world in which Abraham and lot lived, and there are sure battles to fight on many fronts. It is also manifestly clear that great heroes of the faith are sorely needed today, and our God stands ready to aid any willing to stand up for his name.

We need to consider that just as Abraham went to extraordinary lengths to rescue Lot, our saviour went to great lengths to save us. Abraham went out in the knowledge that there was a possibility some would not come back. Our Lord came into this world with the certain knowledge that it would end on a cruel Roman cross.

BSLE: Have we had battles? Are we currently in battles? Have we avoided some battles? How did we feel at the time of the battle?

After his return, Abraham was met by the Valley's kings, and amongst them was Melchizedek, king of Salem. Now, I am a history guy and not a doctrinal guy. This character Melchizedek crosses the boundary from history into doctrinal, and I am not the person to explain him to you, but I would advise you, at some point, to research who he was.

Abraham refused to take any payment of any kind from the kings of the valley as he had sworn an oath that he would not take anything for this adventure from them. It does not record that Abraham had talked or prayed to God before setting out on this adventure, but this mention indicates that he did.

The lesson in this story is that we should always be ready to help our friends, neighbours, colleagues and acquaintances whatever their position. This should be done in knowing that we were once in that position, lost and with no hope. We should always be able to offer hope to the lost in this world and should do it without much thought.

BSLE: Do we remember when we were lost? Did anyone make an extra effort to help us? Should we do the same?

However, in helping those around us, we must be careful not to get involved in the things of the world. Abraham refused any compensation as that was not the reason he carried out this mission. He carried out this mission to save a life, which is the only reward he sought. We must be the same, single-minded in our pursuit of souls for God's kingdom and seeking no other compensation apart from this.

BSLE: Do any group members have any experience of getting too involved with the world?

We often see blurred lines when we look at mega Churches in the USA and the vast personal wealth of those running them. We as Christians are uncomfortable, so how then does it look to those looking in. Of course, we need to cover expenses, and this is precisely what Abraham did, he accepted what it had cost them to feed the men and the share due to those who were to be paid, but he received nothing for himself. Let this be our example.

BSLE: Discuss this chapter in general and make sure your students fully understand it. Reinforce the need to rely on God when we face battles. Discuss giving to the Church and our position in this matter.

Finally, encourage your group to read the next chapter before meeting again.

CHAPTER 7

A Son Promised

A Son Promised
Genesis Ch 15 v 1-6
After this, the word of the Lord came to Abram in a vision:
"Do not be afraid, Abram. I am your shield, your very great reward."
But Abram said, "Sovereign Lord, what can you give me since I remain childless and the one who will inherit my estate is Eliezer of Damascus?" And Abram said, "You have given me no children; so a servant in my household will be my heir."
Then the word of the Lord came to him: "This man will not be your heir, but a son who is your own flesh and blood will be your heir." He took him outside and said, "Look up at the sky and count the stars—if indeed you can count them." Then he said to him, "So shall your offspring be." Abram believed the Lord, and he credited it to him as righteousness.

Abraham was indeed favoured of God, and once again, we see God coming to communicate directly with him. However, it seems Abraham is still struggling to understand God's plan for his life. I don't think it was so much unbelief, but rather a difficulty understanding what God was saying to him.

God had told him that his descendants would be like the dust of the earth, an excellent promise, but I think Abraham was having difficulty visualising this. People didn't have children when they were in their eighties. It just didn't happen, so what could God possibly be saying.

BSLE: Discuss things in our lives or in our Church that seem impossible, yet also seem as though they are the will of God.

Abraham seems to have thought this through and concluded that his servant Eliezer would be his heir so that this is how God would work out his plans. This is something which we all do at times. We take a spiritual solution and try to fit it into an earthly understanding, which does not work out. Sometimes our head just gets a block, and we cannot see how God can work things out as we are considering earthly restrictions when all that is called for is simple faith.

God then corrects Abraham's thinking. Abraham is told that his descendants will not come from his servant but will come from his own body. Abraham is quick to accept this and believes God implicitly, and his faith is counted as righteousness.

BSLE: Tease out this subject a little more if required and focus on the impossible things your group just can't see how it will work out.

This principle that faith is counted as righteousness is crucial to understanding the Christian doctrine. Many people in the world, even within the Church, can't get their heads around that acceptance and faith are what it is all about. They somehow feel the need to do something, but there is nothing we can do in truth. Adding on something on top of what Jesus has done is an insult to God.

As we read through scripture, it is obvious that God loves a person who quite simply takes him at his word, and this type of person can be used by God more often. God cannot use someone who continually tries to add something extra to the mix. Abraham has done this at times, but overall, his faith in God is unshakeable.

BSLE: Discuss faith and what it is. Particularly how faith leads to actions, usually before you see results.

We are now at a point in our Christian lives where we are in communion with God, and we have read and examined God's promises. We believe that God can work in our lives to produce fruit and bring new sinners to repentance through our life and witness, but somehow, we do not yet visualise precisely how he will do this.

There is a thought that God will do this through his Church, and we will be part of it. There is no real thought that we are the main lead in this process. Our thought process is that someone else will be blessed, someone else will be chosen to carry out the work, and someone else will be a faithful minister who will go out there and bring in the sheaves.

We need to stop right there and consider this passage. If that is where we are in our journey, then we need to hear the words of God. "This man will not be your heir., but one who shall come forth from your own body shall be your heir".

No one else will be the one who will be blessed, do the work or be a faithful minister. God has chosen you, and he asks you to look up at the night sky and consider the stars. The believers who come to faith because of your faith will be like the stars of the sky.

BSLE: Are you somewhere you can take your students outside and have a look at the night sky? Do it. If not, have a picture of the stars handy. Discuss the majestic stars and how God made every one of them. Bring the ending of the discussion round to the promise in front of us. If we step out in faith, our result will be the same as Abraham.

How many sons of promise did Abraham see in his lifetime? Only one! That is irrelevant. The promise may not be for an immediate result, but Abraham believed God, counted unto him as righteousness. Do we believe in God's promise to us?

Edward Kimball was a Sunday School teacher in Boston in 1855 and talked to a boy about how much God loved him. The boy accepted

Christ as his saviour, and for all we know, may be the only convert Edward Kimball led to the Lord. Edward Kimball said of the boy, "I can truly say, and in saying it I magnify the infinite grace of God as bestowed upon him, that I have seen few persons whose minds were spiritually darker than was his when he came into my Sunday School class; and I think that the committee of the Mount Vernon Church seldom met an applicant for membership more unlikely ever to become a Christian of clear and decided views of Gospel truth, still less to fill any extended sphere of public usefulness."

We carry out God's work for us, and we believe that God will use the work we do, not knowing how it will all work out. The boy above, who looked very unlikely to Edward Kimball, was none other than D. L. Moody, the great evangelist who led thousands upon thousands to Christ. These thousands upon thousands are a direct result of Edward Kimball's faithfulness to teach at Sunday school. Let us carry out our work for the Lord faithfully, believing in the harvest to come.

BSLE: Discuss the chapter in general and reinforce the importance of faith. Talk about other examples of faith in your local area, if possible.

Finally, encourage your group to read the next chapter before meeting again.

CHAPTER 8

The Covenant

The Covenant
Genesis Ch 15 v 7 to 18

He also said to him, "I am the Lord, who brought you out of Ur of the Chaldeans to give you this land to take possession of it."

But Abram said, "Sovereign Lord, how can I know that I will gain possession of it?"

So the Lord said to him, "Bring me a heifer, a goat and a ram, each three years old, along with a dove and a young pigeon."

Abram brought all these to him, cut them in two and arranged the halves opposite each other; the birds, however, he did not cut in half. Then birds of prey came down on the carcasses, but Abram drove them away.

As the sun was setting, Abram fell into a deep sleep, and a thick and dreadful darkness came over him. Then the Lord said to him, "Know for certain that for four hundred years your descendants will be strangers in a country not their own and that they will be enslaved and mistreated there. But I will punish the nation they serve as slaves, and afterward they will come out with great possessions. You, however, will go to your ancestors in peace and be buried at a good old age. In the fourth generation your de-

scendants will come back here, for the sin of the Amorites has not yet reached its full measure."

When the sun had set and darkness had fallen, a smoking fire pot with a blazing torch appeared and passed between the pieces. On that day the Lord made a covenant with Abram and said, "To your descendants I give this land, from the Wadi of Egypt to the great river, the Euphrates.

Faith is always rewarded with God. Faith is a pleasing response to God, and he blesses those who have complete faith in him. Once again, God communicates with Abraham and confirms that he is giving this land to Abraham and his descendants.

I guess this another of these areas where Abraham believes in God but cannot begin to figure out how it will happen. Perhaps Abraham is thinking over the next few years or decades, and God must show him that he is looking at a much longer timescale, looking ahead over four hundred years.

BSLE: It is OK if we do not fully understand how God will work out his plan, but we must have a simple belief. Discuss God's timeframe compared to ours.

God decides to make an official covenant with Abraham, which would be for Abraham's benefit, not his own. During this event, Abraham falls into a deep sleep and receives a vision of what is to be. The image is not very pleasant, but God holds nothing back from Abraham, showing him what is to come to pass for his descendants. He also shows him some of what will happen in his own life, telling him that he will live to a ripe old age and be buried in peace.

What view or vision do we have of the work of God in our lives? Is our faith accepting and straightforward, or do we try to assess it in earthly terms? Do we realise that the plan which God has for us could be for longer than our lifetime and that we may not necessarily see the fruits of our labours in person?

BSLE: This is an excellent time to discuss again the vision God has given each of your group. Perhaps you need to relate to the written record you kept. Has it changed? Has it developed? Is the faith of the group growing?

If we have accepted Christ as our Lord and saviour, then we are also covered by a covenant, but it is a new covenant that Jesus himself instituted. The Lord's supper represented the new covenant, the bread which represents his body broken for us and the wine which represents his blood shed for us. The details of this new covenant are fascinating but not within my remit in this book.

In the covenant that God made with Abraham, he detailed the land granted to Abraham's descendants. They would stretch from the river Nile in Egypt in the west to the river Euphrates in the east.

This is very interesting as the land of Israel, even at its most significant, was nowhere near these boundaries. It did, however, leave no room for doubt in Abraham's mind. God had mapped out the exact boundaries of the land his descendants would inherit. It leaves some questions for us though, as we consider when and how this expansion will come to pass. Like Abraham, we can only take God at his word and marvel at his command of the heavens and the earth.

For us in our Christian journey, we need to confront the reality that the promise may be beyond our earthly lifespan, but that nevertheless, we need to learn to accept God at his word and believe his promises.

We also need to accept that there may be dark periods ahead of us and that this also is part of God's plan. When trials and troubles come upon us, this is not the end of God's plan or God's work. It is merely part of the plan. God now tells Abraham of Joseph going down into Egypt, which does not look all that good, but for us looking back, we can see how a great nation grew out of the 70 persons who went down into Egypt and how, when the time was right, they came back to fulfil God's promise to Abraham.

Let us consider the long term and care not whether we see results. Let us steadfastly believe in the word of God that He will reward us if we are faithful. Let us be faithful to begin the work God has for us, believing that the harvest will come. Let us start acting as though it is already happening.

BSLE: Continue the discussion on faith and lead onto the covenant God made with Abraham. Lead from this covenant onto the new covenant, and it may be good to remember the Lord in communion, depending on your group's makeup. Dwell on the death, resurrection and ascension of our Lord and his position now, intervening for us.

Finally, encourage your group to read the next chapter before meeting again.

CHAPTER 9

Shortcuts in the Faith

Shortcuts in the Faith
Genesis Ch 16 v1-6

Now Sarai, Abram's wife, had borne him no children. But she had an Egyptian slave named Hagar; so she said to Abram, "The Lord has kept me from having children. Go, sleep with my slave; perhaps I can build a family through her."

Abram agreed to what Sarai said. So after Abram had been living in Canaan ten years, Sarai his wife took her Egyptian slave Hagar and gave her to her husband to be his wife. He slept with Hagar, and she conceived.

When she knew she was pregnant, she began to despise her mistress. Then Sarai said to Abram, "You are responsible for the wrong I am suffering. I put my slave in your arms, and now that she knows she is pregnant, she despises me. May the Lord judge between you and me."

"Your slave is in your hands," Abram said. "Do with her whatever you think best." Then Sarai mistreated Hagar; so she fled from her.

Abraham was still trying to come to terms with how God could grant him a son. God had promised him that it would be his son, but obviously, he was still having problems accepting this, and instead of just waiting to see God work his wonders, he felt he needed to take some action to help it along. Sarah suggested a solution, and Abraham, for once he did not consult God on this matter but proceeded with Sarah's plan to produce offspring through her maid, Hagar.

I guess in Abraham's mind, this solution did not contradict God's plan as this would be his child, fulfilling God's word. Why would Abraham, who was so close to God, fail to consult God this time? The answer seems to carry a similarity to the events in the garden of Eden, where Satan firstly corrupted Eve and used her to waylay Adam. Here we see Satan use the same strategy to confuse and cause an error, firstly convincing Sarah that there was an answer to her problem which did not concern God. He then used Sarah to persuade Abraham to carry out her plan.

The problems this error produced are still affecting us today as we see great turmoil between Abraham's descendants through Ishmael in constant adversity against the nation of Israel. We must be careful not to try and force God's plan. Going down the wrong route can cause massive problems, not only for us but for generations to come.

BSLE: Have any within our group taken shortcuts to God's plan? How did that work out?

Sarah conceived the plan, and then when it all went wrong, she blamed Abraham for the outcome. We can only view this as a monumental mistake in Abraham's life, which has had severe consequences for the last four thousand years. What lessons are we to draw from this episode, and what part of our journey does this represent.

You will remember, we talked about Egypt representing the world, and here we find Abraham getting involved with an Egyptian woman, so Abraham is getting involved with the world. How many times in our lives and our Churches do we get involved in the world?

BSLE: Do we see any ways in which our Church or we are getting involved with the world?

Many Churches these days are more akin to social clubs and get involved in all sorts of worldly things. A look through the adverts in any local paper will show you Churches having jumble sales, darts nights, quizzes, entertainments, ecumenical meetings with false religions, and all sorts of things. While all these things may not always be wrong on their own, you will find that they have no prayer meeting because no one is interested in attending.

Many Churches have become so involved with the world that they live the same way as the world. They are part of the world. We are called on to be different from the world, to be separate from the world for a good reason. If we have nothing different from the world, why would the world be interested in us? There are loads of clubs out there. Why would they be interested in one more?

We must be in the world, but not of the world. We must be the light of the world, and we must be the salt of the earth. God's original plan has not changed. He chose Abraham to build a nation, and now that nation includes us. His plan for that nation was to bless all the nations of the earth. To do this, we must stand out from the other nations and not become entangled with them.

BSLE: Discuss this chapter in general and show a clear difference between the world and the Church. Is this always easy? Reinforce the need always to keep communications with God open. If we are not praying about it, something is wrong.

Finally, encourage your group to read the next chapter before meeting again.

CHAPTER 10

Circumcision

Circumcision
Genesis Ch 17 v 1 to 14

When Abram was ninety-nine years old, the Lord appeared to him and said, "I am God Almighty; walk before me faithfully and be blameless. Then I will make my covenant between me and you and will greatly increase your numbers."

Abram fell facedown, and God said to him, "As for me, this is my covenant with you: You will be the father of many nations. No longer will you be called Abram; your name will be Abraham, for I have made you a father of many nations. I will make you very fruitful; I will make nations of you, and kings will come from you. I will establish my covenant as an everlasting covenant between me and you and your descendants after you for the generations to come, to be your God and the God of your descendants after you. The whole land of Canaan, where you now reside as a foreigner, I will give as an everlasting possession to you and your descendants after you; and I will be their God."

Then God said to Abraham, "As for you, you must keep my covenant, you and your descendants after you for the generations to come. This is my covenant with you and your descendants after you, the covenant you are to keep: Every male among you shall be circumcised. You are to undergo circumcision, and it will be the sign of the covenant between me and you. For the generations to come every male among you who is eight days old must be circumcised, including those born in your household or bought with money from a foreigner—those who are not your offspring. Whether born in your household or bought with your money, they must be circumcised. My covenant in your flesh is to be an everlasting covenant. Any uncircumcised male, who has not been circumcised in the flesh, will be cut off from his people; he has broken my covenant."

We pick up the story of Abraham a further thirteen years down the line, and once again, God comes to talk to him. We do not know what has happened in the intervening thirteen years, but God was pleased with Abraham. So much so that he confirms his covenant and promises much more than before.

God had promised Abraham that his descendants would be numerous and a great nation until this point. Now God is promising that it would not be one nation, but many nations and history has borne this out. The entire middle east is descendent from Abraham.

BSLE: Over the years, has God expanded our vision?

As God confirms the covenant, he also institutes a sign of the covenant in the form of circumcision. All male descendants of Abraham are to be circumcised on the eighth day. This is still practised today by Jews and Arabs, who are also descendent of Abraham. It is not only a religious ritual, but it is also proven as a health benefit in many ways.

Long before anyone ever knew anything about the health benefits, perhaps God was instigating this procedure to protect his people. It is also practised widely in the USA, but not in Europe.

We do not know why God introduced this practice, but for Abraham, it was enough to obey and comply with God's wishes. Abraham had reached the point where he trusted God completely and had learned not to query the reasons. God considered it a serious matter. Anyone not circumcised should have no part of this people and would be deemed to have broken the covenant and therefore denounced the benefits and promises.

Significantly, circumcision was suspended for the forty years the Israelites wandered in the desert after leaving Egypt. This is linked to unbelief when the people refused to enter the promised land due to fear. Forty years later, circumcision was restored when the people eventually came to enter their inheritance. Circumcision was a sign that the people were under God's covenant.

We in the Church are under a new covenant and no longer require physical circumcision, but we still need circumcision of our heart. In Deuteronomy Ch 30 v 6, Moses says, "Moreover, the Lord your God will circumcise your heart and the heart of your descendants, to love the Lord your God with all your heart and with all your soul, in order that you may live."

Note that God will carry out the circumcision, not us. This is done in the same way as our salvation. It is the work of Christ that we could never hope to accomplish ourselves. God knows our weaknesses and our failings. Before choosing us as his own, he knew we would continually fail him. The important thing is not the letter of the law and being a 'goody two shoes', but the heart. King David had many failings and made many mistakes, but God said that he was a man after his own heart, which mattered most.

In Colossians Ch 2, Paul addresses this issue. He says, "See to it that no one takes you captive through philosophy and empty deception, according to the tradition of men, according to the elementary principles of the world, rather than according to Messiah.

For in Him all the fullness of Deity dwells in bodily form.

And in Him you were also circumcised with a circumcision made without hands, in the removal of the body of the flesh by the circumcision of Messiah.

Having been buried with Him in baptism (of the Spirit), in which you were also raised up with Him through faith in the working of God, who raised Him from the dead.

And when you were dead in your transgressions and the uncircumcision of your flesh, He made you alive together with Him, having forgiven us all our transgressions."

Many things have changed between the old covenant and the new, but one thing remains the same. The thing most important to God is our faith and our heart. Everything else will follow.

BSLE: This is a difficult passage and subject, and no doubt many questions will come up concerning the difference between the old and new covenant. Remember that the old covenant was a school teacher to bring us to the new covenant. Even in the old testament, faith was what it was all about.

Finally, encourage your group to read the next chapter before meeting again.

CHAPTER 11

The promise of a Son Affirmed

The Promise of a Son Affirmed
Genesis Ch 17 v 15 to 22

God also said to Abraham, "As for Sarai your wife, you are no longer to call her Sarai; her name will be Sarah. I will bless her and will surely give you a son by her. I will bless her so that she will be the mother of nations; kings of peoples will come from her."

Abraham fell facedown; he laughed and said to himself, "Will a son be born to a man a hundred years old? Will Sarah bear a child at the age of ninety?" And Abraham said to God, "If only Ishmael might live under your blessing!"

Then God said, "Yes, but your wife Sarah will bear you a son, and you will call him Isaac. I will establish my covenant with him as an everlasting covenant for his descendants after him. And as for Ishmael, I have heard you: I will surely bless him; I will make him fruitful and will greatly increase his numbers. He will be the father of twelve rulers, and I will make him into a great nation. But my covenant I will establish with Isaac, whom

Sarah will bear to you by this time next year." When he had finished speaking with Abraham, God went up from him.

Thirteen years on, and obviously, Abraham is still of the mind that Ishmael is his heir and is convinced that now there will be no more children. It, therefore, comes as a shock when God tells him that Sarah will have a son and Abraham's response is to fall on his face and laugh. We would call that rolling on the floor laughing (ROTFL) these days.

God is very explicit in his information and instructions. He informs Abraham that Sarah would become the mother of nations, mirroring Abraham's promise. Abraham is even instructed to name his son Isaac and told that the covenant God had made with Abraham would be confirmed through Isaac. God even informed the rough time of the child's birth as one year on.

BSLE: We are, once again, back on the subject of faith. It is so important to God that it keeps cropping up. Isn't it amazing how difficult it can be for us to believe in God sometimes?

Looking back and reading this in the book of Genesis, it is easy for us to read it and accept it, but can you imagine how Abraham's head must have been spinning. This was something well out of the ordinary and unheard of before. It is easy for us to say that Abraham should have faith, but how would our faith stand up if God were to come to us when we were one hundred years old and were to be a father again, by a wife who was ninety?

In the Christian life, we will come up against such times when our faith will be tested, and it would be well for us to come back to these chapters and remind ourselves that God can do the impossible. That is one of the most important reasons for reading our Bible. We need to be constantly reminded that God can do miracles.

God was looking to do a mighty work here through Abraham. It was a work that was to last through eternity. It was to be a work that would be the backbone of God's plan of redemption. This could not be done, starting from a doubtful liaison position with the world. This work could not be accomplished through worldly intervention. The work of ages must be founded in a pure relationship.

BSLE: We need to be reminded that if God is to do any work through us, then it must come from the proper base of faith and commitment.

This should be a reminder to us as Christians to seek after that which is pure. God cannot use any toxic relationship with the world to the same degree and in the same way. Everything we do in our lives must be done with God's plan in mind, not just running off and doing our own thing. Wrong decisions and turnings in our life make for an ineffective Christian and wasted life, and I have learned this from bitter experience.

If we have gone down wrong paths and waste part of our lives, it is not, however, the end of our usefulness. We must return to God and accept that we seek after that which is pure, and then God can work out his plans in our lives, regardless of how much time we have wasted or how old we are.

BSLE: Have any of your group had wasted years? Discuss this in detail and how you feel about it. Discuss the chapter in general and make sure your students understand the principles of faith.

Finally, encourage your group to read the next chapter before meeting again.

CHAPTER 12

The Angels

The Angels
Genesis Ch 18 v 1-15

The Lord appeared to Abraham near the great trees of Mamre while he was sitting at the entrance to his tent in the heat of the day. Abraham looked up and saw three men standing nearby. When he saw them, he hurried from the entrance of his tent to meet them and bowed low to the ground.

He said, "If I have found favor in your eyes, my lord, do not pass your servant by. Let a little water be brought, and then you may all wash your feet and rest under this tree. Let me get you something to eat, so you can be refreshed and then go on your way—now that you have come to your servant."

"Very well," they answered, "do as you say."

So Abraham hurried into the tent to Sarah. "Quick," he said, "get three seahs of the finest flour and knead it and bake some bread."

Then he ran to the herd and selected a choice, tender calf and gave it to a servant, who hurried to prepare it. He then brought some curds and milk and the calf that had been prepared, and set these before them. While they ate, he stood near them under a tree.

"Where is your wife Sarah?" they asked him.

"There, in the tent," he said.

Then one of them said, "I will surely return to you about this time next year, and Sarah your wife will have a son."

Now Sarah was listening at the entrance to the tent, which was behind him. Abraham and Sarah were already very old, and Sarah was past the age of childbearing. So Sarah laughed to herself as she thought, "After I am worn out and my lord is old, will I now have this pleasure?"

Then the Lord said to Abraham, "Why did Sarah laugh and say, 'Will I really have a child, now that I am old?' Is anything too hard for the Lord? I will return to you at the appointed time next year, and Sarah will have a son."

Sarah was afraid, so she lied and said, "I did not laugh."

But he said, "Yes, you did laugh."

Yet again, God visits Abraham. There is some debate who these three men are, but the consensus is that it may be Jesus and two angels. Regardless of who it is, the message is from God and reiterates what Abraham was told a few weeks prior.

There is little doubt that Abraham and Sarah are flustered by this visit. It would seem they may have been caught unawares, and they rush around to welcome and provide for their guests. Abraham is very insistent that he provides the very best.

Abraham considers at least one of the men to be far superior to himself as he bows himself to the ground. The picture here is not a small curt bow but prostrating himself in the presence of a far greater person.

When everything is prepared and seated, the message is delivered again that Sarah is to have a child in one year. I guess it was protocol, but Sarah left the men to talk, and she stayed in the tent, but she was intent on hearing what was said and was eavesdropping from just inside the door.

Once again, Abraham is told about the child Sarah would have, and when Sarah, listening at the door, heard this, she laughed, but not out loud, just inwardly. Nothing is hidden from God, though, as he can listen to an inward laugh just as well as an outward one. He asked Abraham why Sarah had laughed, which must have seemed strange to Abraham, as he wouldn't have heard anything. Sarah, however, was afraid when she knew she had been found out and denied it.

This reminds us of the garden of Eden again when Adam and Eve tried to deny wrongdoing to God then. We would all do well to remember that nothing is hidden from God. When we consider some of the things we think and do, believing no one sees them, it is chilling to know that God sees right into the very depth of our hearts and fathoms out every thought.

It would seem that God wants to impress on Abraham that nothing is too hard for him to do, and indeed, he tells him exactly that. God is building a nation of his people here, and these people need to be able to look back to the father of their nation and see the greatness of God at work. This means that Abraham's faith must grow stronger yet, and to do that, it has to be further tested. God is pushing the boundaries of Abraham's faith at every point to leave his people with a great example on which to look back.

BSLE: Christians who have been on the road for quite some time may think they have arrived in the faith, but not so. Make sure that your students understand that our faith will always need to be developed further, and the more that God has for us to do, the greater faith we will need.

We come to a point in our Christian life, and we feel that God has finished with us. We have been at the heart of God's work and may have stepped back and just coasting along. Our feeling is that God has done his work through us, and it has ended. The truth is that our work as a Christian is never done until God calls us home, and we must always be ready to look out for the next call of God.

We may well feel that we are old and washed up. We may feel tired or even just out of touch with a younger generation. Undoubtedly, we will get to a point where we think the world has passed us by and that God can no longer possibly have any use for us. We must always keep seeking the face of God, and soon enough, we will see that there are still fields, white to the harvest and still too few workers.

We should recall the parable of the master of the vineyard, that even at the eleventh hour, he was still looking for workers for his vineyard. Even in the eleventh hour of our lives, it is never a time to rest. God will call us home when it is time to rest, but we must be concerned about our Father's things until then.

BSLE: Discuss the chapter in general and answer questions. Note how faith is becoming the dominant requirement.

Finally, encourage your group to read the next chapter before meeting again.

CHAPTER 13

Destruction of Sodom and Gomorrah

Destruction of Sodom and Gomorrah
Genesis Ch 18 v 16 to 33

When the men got up to leave, they looked down toward Sodom, and Abraham walked along with them to see them on their way. Then the Lord said, "Shall I hide from Abraham what I am about to do? Abraham will surely become a great and powerful nation, and all nations on earth will be blessed through him. For I have chosen him, so that he will direct his children and his household after him to keep the way of the Lord by doing what is right and just, so that the Lord will bring about for Abraham what he has promised him."

Then the Lord said, "The outcry against Sodom and Gomorrah is so great and their sin so grievous that I will go down and see if what they have done is as bad as the outcry that has reached me. If not, I will know."

The men turned away and went toward Sodom, but Abraham remained standing before the Lord. Then Abraham approached him and said: "Will you sweep away the righteous with the wicked? What if there are fifty righteous people in the city? Will you really sweep it away and not spare the place for the sake of the fifty righteous people in it? Far be it from you to do such a thing—to kill the righteous with the wicked, treating the righteous and the wicked alike. Far be it from you! Will not the Judge of all the earth do right?"

The Lord said, "If I find fifty righteous people in the city of Sodom, I will spare the whole place for their sake."

Then Abraham spoke up again: "Now that I have been so bold as to speak to the Lord, though I am nothing but dust and ashes, what if the number of the righteous is five less than fifty? Will you destroy the whole city for lack of five people?"

"If I find forty-five there," he said, "I will not destroy it."

Once again he spoke to him, "What if only forty are found there?"

He said, "For the sake of forty, I will not do it."

Then he said, "May the Lord not be angry, but let me speak. What if only thirty can be found there?"

He answered, "I will not do it if I find thirty there."

Abraham said, "Now that I have been so bold as to speak to the Lord, what if only twenty can be found there?"

He said, "For the sake of twenty, I will not destroy it."

Then he said, "May the Lord not be angry, but let me speak just once more. What if only ten can be found there?"

He answered, "For the sake of ten, I will not destroy it."

When the Lord had finished speaking with Abraham, he left, and Abraham returned home.

Carrying on from the same meeting, the three men rise as if to go but hesitate and look towards Sodom. They then tell Abraham about their real reason for being here and plan to destroy Sodom. Two of the men depart towards Sodom and Abraham is left with the one we presume to be Jesus.

Abraham is very agitated, knowing that his nephew Lot is in the city about to be destroyed and tries to bargain with God to spare the city. He starts asking if God would spare the city if there were fifty good men in it and finishes up asking if God would spare it for ten good men. God said that he would spare the entire city if there were ten good men found in it, but Abraham knew in his heart that there were not ten good men in Sodom.

At this point, God departs, and Abraham returns to his tent, no doubt, very distressed. We remember when Abraham heard of Lot being taken captive and how he jumped into action, but this time there was no such option.

BSLE: Are we concerned about the lost we see around us? Does it agitate us that our friends are backslidden?

As Christians, we are often faced with the reality that the ways of God do not mean as much to our children as they do to us and that our children are going astray. When they are young, we try our best to teach them God's ways, but once they are a little older and independent, we often feel pretty helpless and feel we can do little but pray.

Abraham had prayed directly to God for Sodom, but although he had not mentioned Lot, God knew exactly what was in his heart. Although Abraham could not see a solution to the problem, God always has a solution, and we just need to pour out our hearts to him and leave with him. We must never forget what Paul says in Romans Ch8 v1, "All things work together towards good for those who love the Lord".

BSLE: Big takeaway here. Sometimes God has solutions we could never imagine. We must pour out our hearts to him and leave him to be the judge of what is best.

We will not read the passage on the destruction of Sodom and the saving of Lot and his daughters. We have already covered that in the study of Lot. If you haven't read that study, I would urge you to get it as it is a fascinating study of a man who is not so faithful as Abraham.

We must take an important lesson from this passage, though. There will be those God places under our care. It may be our children, or it may be younger Christians we are discipling. The time will come when they move on and do their own thing. We are still called to care for them, though, and they should always be in our prayers and minds.

It may well be that we are not in their minds, but that is unimportant. As in the case of Lot, it may well be that we are very concerned by the route they are taking, and we feel helpless to correct them or turn them in the right direction. This all needs to be taken to God in prayer as he understands the deep longings of our hearts, even the longings we cannot put into words.

BSLE: Discuss family and friends we are concerned about. Discuss how we should bring them to God.

God has an exceedingly high level of love and care for all his children, and it pains him to see his children in unease. If it hurts us, then it hurts our heavenly father. If we are in God's will, like in this situation, God will not hide anything from us but will reveal all. God's intentions may concern us greatly, but they should equip us with the desire and the knowledge and a burden to pray more effectively.

We must never try to change God's plan or plead against God's will. God will work out his plan, and if we make our concerns known to him, he will work out the just solution to our heart cry. This does not mean we never plead with God. Of course we do, and there are numerous examples of this throughout the Bible apart from this one, but at the end of the day, we need to accept that God is sovereign and his ways are far superior to ours.

We recall how Moses pleaded for the Children of Israel in the desert when God declared his intention to wipe them all out and start again with Moses. Moses intervened, and God listened to him. This is proof that God listens and grants the requests of his faithful children and that we are justified in pleading our hearts desires before him.

BSLE: Discuss the entire chapter and answer any questions which arise. Take careful note of any of your group who are agitated about family or friends.

Finally, encourage your group to read the next chapter before meeting again.

CHAPTER 14

The Great Man Stumbles Again

The Great Man Stumbles Again
Genesis Ch 20 v1 to 18

Now Abraham moved on from there into the region of the Negev and lived between Kadesh and Shur. For a while he stayed in Gerar, and there Abraham said of his wife Sarah, "She is my sister." Then Abimelek king of Gerar sent for Sarah and took her.

But God came to Abimelek in a dream one night and said to him, "You are as good as dead because of the woman you have taken; she is a married woman."

Now Abimelek had not gone near her, so he said, "Lord, will you destroy an innocent nation? Did he not say to me, 'She is my sister,' and didn't she also say, 'He is my brother'? I have done this with a clear conscience and clean hands."

Then God said to him in the dream, "Yes, I know you did this with a clear conscience, and so I have kept you from sinning against me. That is why I did not let you touch her. Now return the man's wife, for he is a prophet, and he will pray for you and you will live. But if you do not return her, you may be sure that you and all who belong to you will die."

Early the next morning Abimelek summoned all his officials, and when he told them all that had happened, they were very much afraid. Then Abimelek called Abraham in and said, "What have you done to us? How have I wronged you that you have brought such great guilt upon me and my kingdom? You have done things to me that should never be done." And Abimelek asked Abraham, "What was your reason for doing this?"

Abraham replied, "I said to myself, 'There is surely no fear of God in this place, and they will kill me because of my wife.' Besides, she really is my sister, the daughter of my father though not of my mother; and she became my wife. And when God had me wander from my father's household, I said to her, 'This is how you can show your love to me: Everywhere we go, say of me, "He is my brother."'"

Then Abimelek brought sheep and cattle and male and female slaves and gave them to Abraham, and he returned Sarah his wife to him. And Abimelek said, "My land is before you; live wherever you like."

To Sarah he said, "I am giving your brother a thousand shekels of silver. This is to cover the offense against you before all who are with you; you are completely vindicated."

Then Abraham prayed to God, and God healed Abimelek, his wife and his female slaves so they could have children again, for the Lord had kept all the women in Abimelek's household from conceiving because of Abraham's wife Sarah.

You may remember back when Abraham had just arrived in Canaan, that he slipped, and his faith faltered. You will recall that Abraham went down to Egypt against the explicit command of God to stay in the land and take possession. We thought that Abraham had learned his lesson from that, but we were wrong.

In this deception, both Abraham and Sarah are complicit. It says something about Sarah, though, at ninety years old, she is still attractive and desirable. God had huge plans for Abraham and Sarah, and she is on the point of conceiving and bearing a son, so this could not be allowed.

BSLE: Have any of your group fallen twice in the same way. The author of this study has. Your students need to know that Satan will never stop attacking them.

Why does Abraham feel so threatened that he has created a deception like this? The feats he has accomplished would lead us to think that Abraham would be afraid of nothing, yet here he is, scared for his life. Is this another test from God, designed to strengthen his faith?

Indeed, these deceptions always seem to make Abraham richer as the kings involved are absolutely terrified and heap treasures upon Abraham just to be rid of him. On this occasion, Abraham has to pray to restore the king and his entire kingdom, who had all become barren and sterile due to this episode.

When we progress through life, there is a sense that we come to a point where we think we are beyond falling. We may come to a point where we feel we need not consult God on every detail of our lives. Abraham and Sarah were at a high point in their lives and months away from the fulfilment of god's promise of a son, and yet, they fall spectacularly from God's grace simply because they did not take a matter they were concerned about to God.

BSLE: Have there been some areas of our lives we do not seek God's guidance on? How did that go?

We have often seen this in the Christian Church too. Many highly effective and influential leaders in the Church have fallen spectacularly, and often we look on without compassion and condemn them. The truth is that the old saying is relevant here, "There, but for the grace of God, go I". None of us is ever beyond the point where we can fall in this life. We continually require help and support from our heavenly father.

BSLE: Discuss a prominent Church leader who has fallen in the past. Do any of us think that could not happen to me?

If we begin to trust in our own abilities, then we have underestimated the power of our adversity, the devil. He will never let up and is always looking for an opportunity to bring leaders in the Church down. He only needs a small chink in our armour to strike a blow, and any matter we fail to take to God takes us further away from his protection.

Apart from learning we must stay close to God, we must also learn that none of us are above falling, and we need to deal with any brother or sister who falls accordingly. If a brother or sister falls, it should hurt us just as if it were ourselves, and we should be ready to help them back up. I have both been the brother who falls and seen others fall in my life. In some ways, it is more hurtful to see another brother fall than if it had been yourself.

In the Church, we are a family of God's children. We should stand ready to help each other whatever the situation. When another family member falls, it reflects on the entire family and hurts us the whole family. Let us bind ourselves together to help each other in every situation.

BSLE: Discuss the chapter in general with an emphasis on how we can help each other, especially those who fall.

Finally, encourage your group to read the next chapter before meeting again.

CHAPTER 15

The Birth of Isaac

The Birth of Isaac
Genesis Ch 21 v 1 to 7
Now the Lord was gracious to Sarah as he had said, and the Lord did for Sarah what he had promised. Sarah became pregnant and bore a son to Abraham in his old age, at the very time God had promised him. Abraham gave the name Isaac to the son Sarah bore him. When his son Isaac was eight days old, Abraham circumcised him, as God commanded him. Abraham was a hundred years old when his son Isaac was born to him.

Sarah said, "God has brought me laughter, and everyone who hears about this will laugh with me." And she added, "Who would have said to Abraham that Sarah would nurse children? Yet I have borne him a son in his old age." The child grew and was weaned, and on the day Isaac was weaned Abraham held a great feast.

Abraham has had to wait a long time for this promise to come true. He is now one hundred years old and Sarah is ninety, long past when they should have been having children. It reminds us somewhat of another miraculous birth which is to take place around two thousand years later, the birth of Jesus himself.

There is great rejoicing in the household at Isaac's birth, and perhaps both Abraham and Sarah are now learning that nothing is beyond the capability of our God. Still, this is one child, and God promised not only an entire nation but many nations would come from these two people. It was still a massive leap of faith to believe God's full promise.

BSLE: Have we seen an answer to promises? What did it feel like? Was that followed by a more significant promise or expectation?

We can look back on our lives and see times when God delivered his promises and recall the times of rejoicing. Times when close friends or family responded to the call of God and accepted Christ as their saviour. We may have seen times of great revival and God moving through entire communities. It may simply be a close encounter with God that no one else knows about apart from ourselves.

Every one of us can look back on life and pick out a time when we have been thrilled with the presence of God in our lives and when we see the plans of God unfolding in miraculous ways. Our salvation is our first experience of this, and usually, the salvation of any soul is another episode of pure joy. The Bible tells us that there is great rejoicing in heaven over one sinner that repents. There was great rejoicing in Abraham's household over one baby being born.

Every believer who is close to God longs for the day that revival will break out and experience the pure joy of seeing many ransomed souls come home. God makes many promises about this in scripture, and we can take these promises as ours. However, these promises are all conditional.

BSLE: Are we praying for revival?

Revival does not depend on the condition of those who are to come to God. Every living man or woman is alien to God and degenerate and can no more come to God than a dead body can rise and walk. Revival starts with the Church who believe in the promises of God. A church that is inward-looking and cares for nothing but the protection of its standards and customs will never experience revival.

To experience revival, a Church must forget about their own needs and be so broken and concerned for the lost around them that they are driven to their knees to call out to God for them. Abraham and Sarah were like this. They cried out to God for a child, and although it was a long time coming, God did answer their prayers.

As a Church, we need to come together and cry out to God for times of revival. God wants to bring sinners home to himself, but do we, the Church? How much do we want it? Are we at the point where we will lay aside everything else in our lives and pursue this? Are we at the point where nothing else matters but reaching the lost and saving them from a lost eternity and separation from God? Are we deeply burdened and concerned for the lost?

When you stand in the street and look around you, what do you see? Do you see ordinary people enjoying and getting on with life, or do you see lost sheep heading for a lost eternity and not even knowing that they are lost? Are there tears in your eyes as you look out over your town or city and contemplate the destination of its inhabitants? Good! It is almost time for a revival!

BSLE: Discuss this chapter and answer questions. Also, initiate discussion on what it will take to get a revival. Is the Church ready for it? Should we be ready? Is that what faith is?

Finally, encourage your group to read the next chapter before meeting again.

CHAPTER 16

The Ishmael Problem

The Ishmael Problem
Genesis Ch 21 v 9 to 21

But Sarah saw that the son whom Hagar the Egyptian had borne to Abraham was mocking, and she said to Abraham, "Get rid of that slave woman and her son, for that woman's son will never share in the inheritance with my son Isaac."

The matter distressed Abraham greatly because it concerned his son. But God said to him, "Do not be so distressed about the boy and your slave woman. Listen to whatever Sarah tells you, because it is through Isaac that your offspring will be reckoned. I will make the son of the slave into a nation also, because he is your offspring."

Early the next morning Abraham took some food and a skin of water and gave them to Hagar. He set them on her shoulders and then sent her off with the boy. She went on her way and wandered in the Desert of Beersheba.

When the water in the skin was gone, she put the boy under one of the bushes. Then she went off and sat down about a bowshot away, for she thought, "I cannot watch the boy die." And as she sat there, she began to sob.

God heard the boy crying, and the angel of God called to Hagar from heaven and said to her, "What is the matter, Hagar? Do not be afraid; God has heard the boy crying as he lies there. Lift the boy up and take him by the hand, for I will make him into a great nation."

Then God opened her eyes and she saw a well of water. So she went and filled the skin with water and gave the boy a drink.

God was with the boy as he grew up. He lived in the desert and became an archer. While he was living in the Desert of Paran, his mother got a wife for him from Egypt.

When we do not follow God's plan in our life, it just leads to trouble, and here we have a classic example. As soon as Isaac is born, there is strife between Isaac and Ishmael and not just a little jealousy on Sarah's part. This is also a lack of faith as God had clearly stated that the inheritance would be through Isaac, so if Sarah had truly believed, she would not have worried about Ishmael usurping Isaac.

Ishmael would have been around fourteen years old at this point, and Abraham seems to have been pretty attached to him, so it created turmoil in Abraham's mind about what to do with this problem. However, God spoke to Abraham again and told Abraham to send Hagar and Ishmael away from him. It seems cruel to us, but God had plans for Ishmael too, but they did not involve remaining with Abraham.

BSLE: Have any of your group got any experience of failings in the past still causing them problems? We need to emphasise God's complete forgiveness.

Hagar and Ishmael went into the desert and wandered around with their water bottles empty when God intervened in their lives too. God provided for them and promised Hagar that a great nation would come from Ishmael.

BSLE: Do your group realise that God also blessed the Arab nations, descendents of Ishmael. What's the difference between being blessed and being under the covenant?

This is a sad episode in the narrative and, unfortunately, caused a lot of bad blood between the two half-brothers. It is bad blood that still causes huge problems around four thousand years later because Abraham took matters into his own hand.

As we go through our Christian lives, we will make mistakes, sometimes big ones. Some of these mistakes will affect us and affect the lives of those around us and even the lives of those not yet born. It is far better in life not to make mistakes, but we need to learn to deal with them once they are made. It is the same path every time. We must take these matters to our Lord, who has the wisdom to deal with these things.

BSLE: This is a complex topic to discuss. Give students an opportunity, but do not push it and be ready to shut it down if a student goes too far. Ask them to talk about it later in private.

Have you ever faced problems in life and do not know which way to go? Every possible route you see open to you looks unattractive and looks like someone will get hurt. You know that this situation is down to you, and you are responsible for putting yourself in this position and others. Satan tells you that you have created this problem so that you are responsible for solving it. He tells you that you have acted outside of God's will, so it is not God's responsibility to sort it out.

Remember that the devil is the father of lies. Do not listen to him, as he will always tell you half-truths. Yes, you are responsible for this situation, but your heavenly Father never abandons you because you fall. Your heavenly father wants to take responsibility for your mistakes and fix them. He knows your weakness and understands and is like any caring father, waiting for you to come and ask for his help.

When you face any heart-breaking situation which you cannot see a way out of, then run to your father in heaven who sees the end from the beginning. He knows what to do, and he will guide you in the direction you should take. There will be consequences, but you know that already. The important thing is to acknowledge that you were outside the will of

God in the past but to ensure now that you seek out and follow the will of God going forward.

Discuss this chapter in general and answer any questions which arise. Be very careful about looking for past problems in the group.

Finally, encourage your group to read the next chapter before meeting again.

CHAPTER 17

The Great Test

The Great Test
Genesis Ch 22 v 1 to 14

Some time later God tested Abraham. He said to him, "Abraham!"
"Here I am," he replied.
Then God said, "Take your son, your only son, whom you love—Isaac—and go to the region of Moriah. Sacrifice him there as a burnt offering on a mountain I will show you."
Early the next morning Abraham got up and loaded his donkey. He took with him two of his servants and his son Isaac. When he had cut enough wood for the burnt offering, he set out for the place God had told him about. On the third day Abraham looked up and saw the place in the distance. He said to his servants, "Stay here with the donkey while I and the boy go over there. We will worship and then we will come back to you."
Abraham took the wood for the burnt offering and placed it on his son Isaac, and he himself carried the fire and the knife. As the two of them went on together, Isaac spoke up and said to his father Abraham, "Father?"
"Yes, my son?" Abraham replied.

"The fire and wood are here," Isaac said, *"but where is the lamb for the burnt offering?"*

Abraham answered, "God himself will provide the lamb for the burnt offering, my son." And the two of them went on together.

When they reached the place God had told him about, Abraham built an altar there and arranged the wood on it. He bound his son Isaac and laid him on the altar, on top of the wood. Then he reached out his hand and took the knife to slay his son. But the angel of the Lord called out to him from heaven, "Abraham! Abraham!"

"Here I am," he replied.

"Do not lay a hand on the boy," he said. "Do not do anything to him. Now I know that you fear God, because you have not withheld from me your son, your only son."

Abraham looked up and there in a thicket he saw a ram caught by its horns. He went over and took the ram and sacrificed it as a burnt offering instead of his son. So Abraham called that place The Lord Will Provide. And to this day it is said, "On the mountain of the Lord it will be provided."

This section certainly seems like a strange story to us, and we are left wondering why a loving God would ask something like this from his children. The truth is that it was a test and was never going to be carried out. Not only this, but it was a necessary lesson for the great things which God had in store for Abraham and his descendants. God had great things ahead of Abraham and his descendants, and a great start was required for subsequent generations to look back on.

Of course, Abraham didn't know this at the time, and it must have been with a heavy heart that he proceeded to carry out this request. However, although Abraham did not know the outcome and what God had planned, he knew in his heart the character of God and reasoned that God had promised that his covenant would be established through Isaac. Therefore, it is complete faith to accept that whatever the outcome, God had pledged the future to Isaac, so would have to perform it, one way or another.

BSLE: Have any in your group been called on to make huge sacrifices? If not, perhaps study someone from history who has to initiate a discussion.

This was the ultimate test for Abraham, and to see how readily he accepted it, is in complete contrast to his unbelief of a few years previously when he pretended Sarah was his sister for fear of death. I often wonder what was going through Isaac's mind as he is tied up and placed on the altar, his father hovering over him with the knife raised.

In a way, this is the situation we were in before we met Jesus. Sin had condemned us, and we were destined for eternal separation from God, with no way out. God is holy, so sin cannot enter his presence. Therefore we could not spend eternity with him. Just as in Isaac's situation, God provided a substitute for us, and we can now be restored to a position of communion with our heavenly Father.

BSLE: Discuss how God provided a substitute for us in our Lord Jesus.

We will have periods of great rejoicing in our Christian lives when God has delivered on his promises. We are close to God and thankful, but we start to take it for granted over time and even start to think it is something we are doing. We may get puffed up with our own importance, and the sad thing is that our human nature always wants to think about how important we are and how well we are doing.

The higher up the chain of leadership, the more the devil attacks and tries to get us to release our reliance on God. He is very wily and knows full well that we can never stand on our own. Sadly, it is a point which most Christians forget from time to time and learn the hard way.

If God has great work for us, he will test our faith to make it stronger. Great works require great faith, and we need to have complete trust in God regardless of whether we understand what he is asking. Sometimes the things God asks may seem crazy to us, but we are simply called to obey. Sometimes God asks tough things, but our faith must be resolute and trust God implicitly that he will remain faithful to his promises. It is only with faith like this that has been tested and tried that God can truly do great works.

BSLE: You must ensure that your students realise that great works only come through great faith and that great faith only comes from significant testing.

When we come through great tests such as Abraham had, the result is the same as Abraham enjoyed. God promises to those who remain faithful that they will be fruitful and see a great blessing, and we see here that this is the only road to real success in the Kingdom of God. If we want to be truly used of God, then we must be prepared to lay everything we have on the altar before him. There must be nothing we will hold back from him.

If we genuinely lay everything on the altar before our God, he will be faithful and reward us greatly. We will see great rewards for our labours in the Kingdom. It will not be worldly rewards as we will already have realised that these matter little. We will have come to a point where we must ask ourselves do we want earthly rewards or to see lost souls come to Jesus. We must choose one or the other. We cannot choose both. Everything we have must be invested into God's kingdom if we want to see revival. There is no other way.

BSLE: Discuss the chapter in-depth and reinforce the message of laying everything on the altar

Finally, encourage your group to read the next chapter before meeting again.

CHAPTER 18

Death of Sarah

Death of Sarah
Genesis Ch 23 v 1 to 20

Sarah lived to be a hundred and twenty-seven years old. She died at Kiriath Arba (that is, Hebron) in the land of Canaan, and Abraham went to mourn for Sarah and to weep over her.

Then Abraham rose from beside his dead wife and spoke to the Hittites. He said, "I am a foreigner and stranger among you. Sell me some property for a burial site here so I can bury my dead."

The Hittites replied to Abraham, "Sir, listen to us. You are a mighty prince among us. Bury your dead in the choicest of our tombs. None of us will refuse you his tomb for burying your dead."

Then Abraham rose and bowed down before the people of the land, the Hittites. He said to them, "If you are willing to let me bury my dead, then listen to me and intercede with Ephron son of Zohar on my behalf so he will sell me the cave of Machpelah, which belongs to him and is at the end of his field. Ask him to sell it to me for the full price as a burial site among you."

Ephron the Hittite was sitting among his people and he replied to Abraham in the hearing of all the Hittites who had come to the gate of his city. "No, my lord," he said. "Listen to me; I give you the field, and I give you the cave that is in it. I give it to you in the presence of my people. Bury your dead."

Again Abraham bowed down before the people of the land and he said to Ephron in their hearing, "Listen to me, if you will. I will pay the price of the field. Accept it from me so I can bury my dead there."

Ephron answered Abraham, "Listen to me, my lord; the land is worth four hundred shekels of silver, but what is that between you and me? Bury your dead."

Abraham agreed to Ephron's terms and weighed out for him the price he had named in the hearing of the Hittites: four hundred shekels of silver, according to the weight current among the merchants.

So Ephron's field in Machpelah near Mamre—both the field and the cave in it, and all the trees within the borders of the field—was deeded to Abraham as his property in the presence of all the Hittites who had come to the gate of the city. Afterward Abraham buried his wife Sarah in the cave in the field of Machpelah near Mamre (which is at Hebron) in the land of Canaan. So the field and the cave in it were deeded to Abraham by the Hittites as a burial site.

At the ripe old age of one hundred and twenty-seven, Sarah died, leaving Abraham and Isaac in his thirties, grieving sorely and unprepared for her burial. It should be noted that at this point, Abraham still did not own even one square inch of the land in which he was living so that he had nowhere to bury his wife.

It is almost comical to read the story of the haggling for a burial site and if we have ever been in a middle eastern marketplace, we will recognise that the manner of dealing has not changed in the past four thousand years. The inhabitants promise that Abraham can have anything he wanted, and it will cost him nothing at all. However, Abraham was old enough and wise enough not to accept something that would not be documented and could also be taken away in the same manner.

I also chuckled when I noted how Ephron threw in a ridiculous price and stated he could never accept such a heavy amount from a friend. Abraham was in no mood to haggle, so he simply handed over the spoken price for the land to bury his wife. Abraham now had his first piece of land in this country to which he had journeyed.

We may well approach the end of our lives and find we have little earthly gains to show for it. Does it matter? We are not of this world; we are only passing through. If we genuinely believe this, then the things of this world will hold little attraction to us compared to God's blessings.

Suppose we can look back at the end of our lives and see that we have been faithful in all things and that we have followed God to the best of our ability and seen the blessings of God poured out, not only on us, but on those around us. Do you suppose that lying on our deathbed will we care how much treasure we have stored up?

Do you believe that how much money we have in the bank will be important to us as we near the end of our lives? As we lie on our deathbeds and look back, what do you suppose our regrets will be? Will it be that we wished we had more money in the bank, or will it be the person we never took the opportunity to talk to, and they are still destined for a lost eternity?

Death and parting are always sad events, but for the Christian, it is only a temporary parting as we have the assurance that we will meet again in our home in heaven, where we will spend eternity in the presence of our great God. To the Christian, death is simply a gateway to life. We are moving on from this temporary dwelling to our permanent home. That does not mean we should not mourn our departing friends, but we do not grieve as those in the world mourn, who have no hope beyond the grave.

Let us mourn for our departing brothers and sisters while rejoicing that God has called them home. Let us lament that we are yet to be called home and still long for the day we will be reunited in that bright land beyond the grave. Let our mourning be short, and continue our work for our Lord.

BSLE: This may be a problematic chapter if any of your group has suffered bereavement. At the end of the chapter, we should discuss death and how it relates to us as Christians instead of non-believers. We should also try to discuss how our life should be changed in light of these observations.

Finally, encourage your group to read the next chapter before meeting again.

CHAPTER 19

A Wife for Isaac

A Wife for Isaac
Genesis Ch 24 v 1 to 67

Abraham was now very old, and the Lord had blessed him in every way. He said to the senior servant in his household, the one in charge of all that he had, "Put your hand under my thigh. I want you to swear by the Lord, the God of heaven and the God of earth, that you will not get a wife for my son from the daughters of the Canaanites, among whom I am living, but will go to my country and my own relatives and get a wife for my son Isaac."

The servant asked him, "What if the woman is unwilling to come back with me to this land? Shall I then take your son back to the country you came from?"

"Make sure that you do not take my son back there," Abraham said. "The Lord, the God of heaven, who brought me out of my father's household and my native land and who spoke to me and promised me on oath, saying, 'To your offspring I will give this land'—he will send his angel before you so that you can get a wife for my son from there. If the woman is unwilling to come back with you, then you will be released from this oath of

mine. Only do not take my son back there." So the servant put his hand under the thigh of his master Abraham and swore an oath to him concerning this matter.

Then the servant left, taking with him ten of his master's camels loaded with all kinds of good things from his master. He set out for Aram Naharaim and made his way to the town of Nahor. He had the camels kneel down near the well outside the town; it was toward evening, the time the women go out to draw water.

Then he prayed, "Lord, God of my master Abraham, make me successful today, and show kindness to my master Abraham. See, I am standing beside this spring, and the daughters of the townspeople are coming out to draw water. May it be that when I say to a young woman, 'Please let down your jar that I may have a drink,' and she says, 'Drink, and I'll water your camels too'—let her be the one you have chosen for your servant Isaac. By this I will know that you have shown kindness to my master."

Before he had finished praying, Rebekah came out with her jar on her shoulder. She was the daughter of Bethuel son of Milkah, who was the wife of Abraham's brother Nahor. The woman was very beautiful, a virgin; no man had ever slept with her. She went down to the spring, filled her jar and came up again.

The servant hurried to meet her and said, "Please give me a little water from your jar."

"Drink, my lord," she said, and quickly lowered the jar to her hands and gave him a drink.

After she had given him a drink, she said, "I'll draw water for your camels too, until they have had enough to drink." So she quickly emptied her jar into the trough, ran back to the well to draw more water, and drew enough for all his camels. Without saying a word, the man watched her closely to learn whether or not the Lord had made his journey successful.

When the camels had finished drinking, the man took out a gold nose ring weighing a beka and two gold bracelets weighing ten shekels. Then he asked, "Whose daughter are you? Please tell me, is there room in your father's house for us to spend the night?"

She answered him, "I am the daughter of Bethuel, the son that Milkah bore to Nahor." And she added, "We have plenty of straw and fodder, as well as room for you to spend the night."

Then the man bowed down and worshiped the Lord, saying, "Praise be to the Lord, the God of my master Abraham, who has not abandoned his kindness and faithfulness to my master. As for me, the Lord has led me on the journey to the house of my master's relatives."

The young woman ran and told her mother's household about these things. Now Rebekah had a brother named Laban, and he hurried out to the man at the spring. As soon as he had seen the nose ring, and the bracelets on his sister's arms, and had heard Rebekah tell what the man said to her, he went out to the man and found him standing by the camels near the spring. "Come, you who are blessed by the Lord," he said. "Why are you standing out here? I have prepared the house and a place for the camels."

So the man went to the house, and the camels were unloaded. Straw and fodder were brought for the camels, and water for him and his men to wash their feet. Then food was set before him, but he said, "I will not eat until I have told you what I have to say."

"Then tell us," Laban said.

So he said, "I am Abraham's servant. The Lord has blessed my master abundantly, and he has become wealthy. He has given him sheep and cattle, silver and gold, male and female servants, and camels and donkeys. My master's wife Sarah has borne him a son in her old age, and he has given him everything he owns. And my master made me swear an oath, and said, 'You must not get a wife for my son from the daughters of the Canaanites, in whose land I live, but go to my father's family and to my own clan, and get a wife for my son.'

"Then I asked my master, 'What if the woman will not come back with me?'

"He replied, 'The Lord, before whom I have walked faithfully, will send his angel with you and make your journey a success, so that you can get a wife for my son from my own clan and from my father's family. You will be released from my oath if, when you go to my clan, they refuse to give her to you—then you will be released from my oath.'

"When I came to the spring today, I said, 'Lord, God of my master Abraham, if you will, please grant success to the journey on which I have come. See, I am standing beside this spring. If a young woman comes out to draw water and I say to her, "Please let me drink a little water from your jar," and if she says to me, "Drink, and I'll draw water for your camels too," let her be the one the Lord has chosen for my master's son.'

"Before I finished praying in my heart, Rebekah came out, with her jar on her shoulder. She went down to the spring and drew water, and I said to her, 'Please give me a drink.'

"She quickly lowered her jar from her shoulder and said, 'Drink, and I'll water your camels too.' So I drank, and she watered the camels also.

"I asked her, 'Whose daughter are you?'

"She said, 'The daughter of Bethuel son of Nahor, whom Milkah bore to him.'

"Then I put the ring in her nose and the bracelets on her arms, 48and I bowed down and worshiped the Lord. I praised the Lord, the God of my master Abraham, who had led me on the right road to get the granddaughter of my master's brother for his son. 49Now if you will show kindness and faithfulness to my master, tell me; and if not, tell me, so I may know which way to turn."

Laban and Bethuel answered, "This is from the Lord; we can say nothing to you one way or the other. Here is Rebekah; take her and go, and let her become the wife of your master's son, as the Lord has directed."

When Abraham's servant heard what they said, he bowed down to the ground before the Lord. Then the servant brought out gold and silver jewelry and articles of clothing and gave them to Rebekah; he also gave costly *gifts to her brother and to her mother. Then he and the men who were with him ate and drank and spent the night there.*

When they got up the next morning, he said, "Send me on my way to my master."

But her brother and her mother replied, "Let the young woman remain with us ten days or so; then you may go."

But he said to them, "Do not detain me, now that the Lord has granted success to my journey. Send me on my way so I may go to my master."

Then they said, "Let's call the young woman and ask her about it." So they called Rebekah and asked her, "Will you go with this man?"

"I will go," she said.

So they sent their sister Rebekah on her way, along with her nurse and Abraham's servant and his men. And they blessed Rebekah and said to her, "Our sister, may you increase to thousands upon thousands; may your offspring possess the cities of their enemies."

Then Rebekah and her attendants got ready and mounted the camels and went back with the man. So the servant took Rebekah and left.

Now Isaac had come from Beer Lahai Roi, for he was living in the Negev. He went out to the field one evening to meditate, and as he looked up, he saw camels approaching. Rebekah also looked up and saw Isaac. She got down from her camel and asked the servant, "Who is that man in the field coming to meet us?"

"He is my master," the servant answered. So she took her veil and covered herself.

Then the servant told Isaac all he had done. Isaac brought her into the tent of his mother Sarah, and he married Rebekah. So she became his wife, and he loved her; and Isaac was comforted after his mother's death.

I am sorry this was such an extended reading, but none of it could have been left out, or the story would not be fully understood. With Sarah gone and Abraham now almost one hundred and forty years old, Abraham must have begun to feel his mortality bearing down upon him.

He must have realised that he would have to prepare Isaac for the next chapter of the destiny on which his family were bound.

Isaac needed a wife, but Abraham knew that none of the inhabitants of this land was suitable for Isaac, and their idolatrous ways would corrupt the pure faith with which he had instilled into Isaac. The only solution was to send for a wife for Isaac from his nearest relatives, who lived in Haran, around five hundred miles to the north.

BSLE: Initiate discussion on the importance of having a life partner who loves God. Most likely, some in your group will have bad experiences of this.

The story is an utterly amazing tale and one which those who love a love story would enjoy. What always amazed me was that having just met Rebekah, Isaac took her as his wife and loved her. As if he did not have to think about it, it was something special that God had given to him.

This episode of Abraham's life reinforces to us the importance of not getting involved with the world, and it is not only for us but also for our children. It is vitally important that our children choose a life partner wisely as this can make or break a relationship and work for God. We need a partner who also loves God and understands his ways. If our partner is of the world, then we will always be in conflict when we attempt to carry out the will of God. We simply cannot expect a worldly person to understand some of the things we have seen as we studied the character of Abraham.

As parents, we must do all within our ability to help our children find suitable partners. This is more difficult these days than the days of Abraham, as arranged marriages are a thing of the past. Indeed, guidance from parents is sneered at. I admit this, having experienced first-hand the results of an unequal yoke. I sneered at my parents' approval, and although my marriage lasted thirty-three years, it was a constant struggle, and the consequences of a lousy choice still cause me problems to this day.

BSLE: Any unmarried in your group? Consider praying for them to find the right partner, if appropriate.

As young people, we cannot underestimate the need for this most crucial step in your life to be a matter to be prayed over extensively together. If you and your intended cannot pray together and agree on all things, it will never work and will cause endless heartache for you and others around you.

The Christian walk is not easy, and if you are to prove faithful and valuable, then two people coming together must be a union made in heaven. We see that Abraham and his servant took this very seriously and were very concerned that God would lead them to the correct person.

We see in this story that if God is involved and we follow his lead, then all other things fall into place. The result is a God-honouring marriage that honours God in return and a loving and fruitful relationship that stands the tests of time.

BSLE: Discuss the chapter in detail, emphasising a God-honouring marriage. Ask students to read the next week's passage at home.

CHAPTER 20

Abraham's Death

Abraham's Death
Genesis Ch 25 v 1 to 11

Abraham had taken another wife, whose name was Keturah. She bore him Zimran, Jokshan, Medan, Midian, Ishbak and Shuah. Jokshan was the father of Sheba and Dedan; the descendants of Dedan were the Ashurites, the Letushites and the Leummites. The sons of Midian were Ephah, Epher, Hanok, Abida and Eldaah. All these were descendants of Keturah.

Abraham left everything he owned to Isaac. But while he was still living, he gave gifts to the sons of his concubines and sent them away from his son Isaac to the land of the east.

Abraham lived a hundred and seventy-five years. Then Abraham breathed his last and died at a good old age, an old man and full of years; and he was gathered to his people. His sons Isaac and Ishmael buried him in the cave of Machpelah near Mamre, in the field of Ephron son of Zohar the Hittite, the field Abraham had bought from the Hittites. There Abraham was buried with his wife Sarah. After Abraham's death, God blessed his son Isaac, who then lived near Beer Lahai Roi.

Abraham lived long enough to see his grandchildren Jacob and Esau, before he died at the ripe old age of one hundred and seventy-five. In his final years, Abraham married again and fathered more children, even though he was over one hundred and forty years old.

Abraham hearkened unto God's instructions, though and remembering that the covenant would be confirmed through Isaac, gave generous gifts to all his offspring while he was alive and sent them off, away from Isaac. When he finally died, he was buried alongside his wife Sarah in the cave and land he had bought.

As we grow old, we do not stop living, and we never stop striving for souls for God's kingdom. Abraham had more family, and this is symbolic for us. We look not for family but for souls to be added to God's kingdom. Even when we are old and feeble, we can still tell of God's wonderful ways. Indeed, we have a rich history of God's love and faithfulness to draw on and pass on to the younger generation.

Just as it is comforting for a grandfather to look around his grandchildren, it is equally comforting to look around our Church and see those we have fathered in the faith, and we never grow too old to bring others to know our great God.

As we move into the twilight years of our lives, let the Church become more important to us. Let us spend more time passing on our knowledge and understanding to the younger generation, and let us spend much more time before our God in prayer. If our knees start to get dodgy, we do not need to fall to our knees. We can pray and worship, even lying in our beds. Let us fall naturally into a conversation mode with our heavenly father. After all, we will soon be going home to meet him face-to-face and enjoy his presence forever.

BSLE: This is the end of the study. Discuss this week's reading and discuss Abraham's entire character. If you feel it is too much, then take another week to go over it again.

We do hope this has made a difference in the lives of your group, and we would love to hear how God has used this study to build up his people. Please take the time to let us know how you found the book and any improvements you think should be made to it. Also, please let us know if you have any matters you would like us to pray for.

You can contact us through the website shown on the next page.

Author's Note

Author's Note

This marks the end of the book. If you have enjoyed this book, we would ask you to help us.

1. We would be grateful if you could leave a review of the book on Amazon. These reviews are the lifeblood of my business, and without them, I would have no new customers, and I could no longer write books.
2. I would welcome you to contact us through my author website at www.jamesgwhitelaw.com. I can assure you I am a real person and do not use a pen name. I will answer any questions you have as soon as I am able.
3. Finally, let your friends know that you read my book and enjoyed it on your social media pages.

Thank you for reading the book.

Scripture quotations taken from The Holy Bible, New International Version® NIV®

Copyright © 1973 1978 1984 2011 by Biblica, Inc. ™

Used by permission. All rights reserved worldwide.

www.ingramcontent.com/pod-product-compliance
Lightning Source LLC
Chambersburg PA
CBHW021446080526
44588CB00009B/719